PRAISE FOR
THE GIRLS' Q&A BOOK ON
FRIENDSHIP

"*The Girls' Q&A Book on Friendship* gives really good advice that will help girls handle their conflicts in a way that makes them feel good about themselves."

  —Rosalind Wiseman
   author of *Queen Bees and Wannabes*

"The best resource I've ever seen for addressing real issues in ways that girls can genuinely hear."

  —Deborah Gilboa, M.D. (AKA Ask Dr. G)
   author of *Get the Behavior You Want...*
   Without Being the Parent You Hate!

". . . an invaluable resource for girls navigating their way through the sometimes tricky pathways of friendship."

  —Jennifer Wider, M.D.
   host of weekly radio show *Am I Normal?*
   and co-author of *Got Teens?*

"This is so cool. I can look up my problem and get the answer!"

  —Priscilla, age 8

"This book could earn Annie Fox the Nobel Peace Prize for tempering Girl Warfare!"
> —**Beth Onufrak, Ph.D.**
> founder of DrBethKids.com

". . . written perfectly for young girls navigating the exciting and challenging world of friendships."
> —**Amy Alamar, Ed.D.,** author of
> *Parenting for the GENIUS*

"This book will change not only the way you look at relationships, but how you counsel the kids in your care."
> —**Lynne Kenney, Psy.D.**
> co-author of *Bloom: Helping Children Blossom*

"I wish counselors would read this book, cause they'd understand better what it's like to be in real social situations. It's harder than they think."
> —**Allie,** age 13

"This book is a great way for kids like me to find answers to questions and not feel like we're alone!"
> —**Ellye,** age 10

"This would have been SO helpful back in 5th grade."
> —**Kristin,** age 12

THE GIRLS' Q&A BOOK
ON
FRIENDSHIP

To Mahathi

Annie Fox

OTHER BOOKS BY ANNIE FOX

- The Teen Survival Guide to Dating and Relating

- Too Stressed to Think? A Teen Guide to Staying Sane When Life Makes You Crazy (with Ruth Kirschner)

- Middle School Confidential Book 1: Be Confident in Who You Are

- Middle School Confidential Book 2: Real Friends vs. the Other Kind

- Middle School Confidential Book 3: What's Up with My Family?

- Are You My Friend? A Raymond and Sheila Story

- Are We Lost? A Raymond and Sheila Story

- People Are Like Lollipops

- Teaching Kids to Be Good People: Progressive Parenting for the 21st Century

More at books.AnnieFox.com

THE GIRLS' Q&A BOOK ON FRIENDSHIP

50 Ways to Fix a Friendship Without the DRAMA

By Annie Fox, M.Ed.
Illustrated by Erica De Chavez

Published by
Electric Eggplant
www.ElectricEggplant.com
+1 (415) 534-5437
press@ElectricEggplant.com

ISBN-13: 978-1502353443   ISBN-10: 150235344X

Visit us at GirlsQandA.com

DEDICATION

For all girls, everywhere. May you always *have* real friends. And may you always *be* the kind of friend you want and need.

Friendship Problems & Solutions

1. Why didn't they invite me to join their club?

2. I'm a better friend than she is.

3. She always gets her way.

4. She's nice to me, but not to other people.

5. They don't believe me!

6. My two friends are fighting.

7. She bullied me, but now she needs a friend.

8. She always interrupts me.

9. She broke her promise.

10. I got invited, but my friend didn't.

11. These people are so annoying!

12. I want to help the new girl, but I don't want to get teased.

13. Someone tattled on my friend.

14. They're giving me the Silent Treatment.

INTRODUCTION

Hi! How's it going? I hope everything in your life is happy. If not, maybe you're reading this book because you are having some friendship drama. At one time or another, most girls do. Girls' friendships can be *complicated*.

Sometimes we have so much fun with our friends we wish our time together would never end. But there are times when even best friends have problems and times when you wonder who your real friends are! That's normal, but it can also be upsetting. When we're upset, we don't always know how to make things better and we need help.

Girls have turned to me for friendship help for a long time. Most are teens. Recently I thought, "If I write a book to help younger girls, maybe they will have fewer friendship problems in elementary and middle school."

The Girls' Q&A Friendship Book is filled with real questions from real girls. Some questions will sound so familiar you'll think, "The same thing happened to me!" Even if you've never faced these challenges, you might someday. Then the advice here can help you. Or, if a friend, your sister, or cousin has a friendship issue, you can use this book to help her.

OK, end of introduction. I hope you enjoy the book. Read it on your own or with your favorite adult. You can read it with friends too. When you talk about the problems and solutions in this book, you'll learn about making friendships stronger and more fun.

Take care!

In friendship,

Annie

P.S. In addition to the fifty questions and answers, this book also has friendship advice from older girls and quizzes to help you think about all of this stuff in new ways.

P.P.S. Visit GirlsQandA.com

Q1:

"Why did my friends make a club and not invite me?"

A: Friends don't have to do *everything* together, but friends should always treat each other with respect. When your friends made their club, they might have told each other, "She won't mind not being invited." If they believed that, then they were wrong because you *do* mind. If they knew (deep down) you would be hurt, then they were being *insensitive*. This means *not caring about someone else's feelings*. Real friends don't treat each other that way.

No one likes feeling left out, but don't sit around feeling sorry for yourself. Tell your friends you want to join their club. If they say, "Sure," then you're in. If the answer is "No," then walk away with your head held high. Tell yourself: "If they don't want me in their club, then they're not the kind of friends I want." Take a deep breath, let it out slowly, and look around. Do you see anyone who might be looking for someone to play with? Walk over. Smile. See what happens next. This could be the beginning of a new friendship.

Q2:

"I always treat my friend so much nicer than she treats me!"

A: When one friend is always nicer, it can seem unfair and off-balance, like trying to stand on one foot. After a while you will start to feel wobbly and uncomfortable. You're either going to fall over or put your foot down.

If your friend doesn't treat you like a real friend, then you need to speak up. That's one way to be a better friend to *yourself*. I understand it can be a little scary to tell a friend that you don't like the way she's acting. But if you want to get this friendship balanced again, you're going to have to do it. And you can!

Pick a private place to talk with your friend. (You don't need an audience.) Say something like this, "How come you don't treat me as nicely as I treat you?" If she acts like she doesn't know what you're talking about, give her a real example. Then close your mouth and listen to what she has to say.

Talking about a friendship problem doesn't always fix it, but *not talking* usually keeps things broken.

Q3:

"Why does my friend always get her way and I never do?"

A: Your friend may be a very creative girl whose brain naturally overflows with ideas of things you can do together. Maybe that's why you wanted her as your friend in the first place. Now it sounds like you're fed up because she doesn't listen to your ideas.

A friendship is supposed to be a two-way street. When it starts feeling like everything always goes in one direction, it's no fun. Please talk to your friend about this. If you don't tell her, then how is she supposed to know how you feel? She isn't a mind reader, is she? No. I didn't think so.

The next time she suggests something that you don't feel like doing, you might say, "How about if we do *my* idea today and yours tomorrow?" If she agrees, great. You've worked through a problem by compromising. (Make sure you cooperate with her tomorrow. That's only fair.) If she doesn't want to compromise, then spend less time with her and more time with friends who like to give everyone a turn taking the lead.

Q4:

"A really *cool* girl is always nice to me, but she's mean to other people. Should I be her friend?"

A: If this girl is being mean, then that's not cool. Really cool people are kind and respectful.

Whenever you're uncomfortable with what's happening around you, it's time to ask yourself, "What can I do to make this better?" The right thing to do, which is also the cool thing, is to speak out against meanness whenever you feel it or see it.

You are feeling uncomfortable with your friend's meanness, but maybe you haven't told her yet. You ask, "Should I be her friend?" Well, part of being a friend is telling her the truth instead of pretending you're OK with what she's doing.

Next time she's not being nice to someone, take a deep breath. It will help you feel calmer and braver. Then say this, "Stop. Leave her alone." Your words have power. They will help the person being bullied. They will also give your friend something to think about. If she changes her behavior, great! If not, maybe you should look for a kinder, cooler girl to be your friend.

Q5:

"My friends say I told them something, but I did *not*, and they won't believe me!"

A: It can be really frustrating when people won't believe the truth. I'm wondering why your friends are acting this way. Think for a minute. Have you ever lied to them? If so, you need to apologize and promise not to do it again. Ask for a second chance to prove that you are a trustworthy friend. Then *be* one. That will help rebuild the trust between you and your friends.

If you have never lied to your friends, they may be angry about something else and getting back at you by *pretending* not to believe you. Try to get to the bottom of this. Ask them, "Why don't you believe me?" Listen to what they say. Apologize if you've done something wrong. If you've haven't done anything wrong and the "We don't believe you!" stuff continues, then take a vacation from this friendship. If they ask, "Why aren't you hanging out with us?" then tell the truth. Say, "I need friends I can trust who trust me too."

How to be a Super Friend

"You'll never have a "perfect" friend. So don't think that if your best friend does something wrong, then you'll never be besties again. You will!"
          —Grace, 12

"Best friends get things wrong, but they will fix them. Fake friends pretend nothing happened."
          —Jazmine, 14

"You don't have to be mean to someone if you don't want to be friends with her. Just be nice. It'll mean more to her than you think."
          —Patricia, 12

"Always listen to your friends, and lend a helping hand when you can."
          —Trella, 15

"It's not just your friends that have to make things right if they're wrong. You do, too."
          —Marci, 13

Q6:

"My friends were super close, but now they're trying to wipe each other off the face of the earth. I hate it!"

A: When friends don't get along, it can feel like you're in the middle of someone else's yucky mess. You want your friends to stop fighting, so be a Peacemaker.

Call a meeting. Bring snacks. Tell your friends how their fighting is "tearing you apart" and how you want to help them be friends again. Then follow these steps:

A. Say, "Here are the rules: You each get a chance to say why you're angry. Friend A, you go first. Then it's Friend B's turn."

B. Your job as Peacemaker is to make sure no one interrupts when someone else is talking.

C. After both friends have told their side of the story, say: "Now we know why you're angry at each other. So what can we do to make peace in our friendship?"

D. Share ideas with each other.

E. Make the needed changes.

I hope this helps! If not, spend separate time with each friend.

Q7:

"A girl has bullied me forever. She just got glasses and now people are making fun of *her*. Should I stick up for her?"

A: What a great question! Isn't life interesting the way things can turn around? This girl picked on you, so you might be thinking, "Why should I help her?" The answer is simple: Because she needs a friend right now. Another reason you should help is because you know *exactly* how bad it feels to be teased. If you stand by and let others make fun of her, you'll be unhappy because you'll know, deep inside, that you could have done something to make things better.

The answer to your question is *yes!* Stick up for the girl with the glasses. It's the right thing to do. But you already know that because you've got a hero's heart. Otherwise, it wouldn't bother you that people are making fun of her.

If you help her, maybe she'll learn something important about respect and kindness. Then who knows? This may be the beginning of a great new friendship!

Q8:

"Whenever I talk, my friend interrupts me!"

A: OMG!! Some people get sooo excited they just can't stop interrupting people! Sounds like your friend, huh?

We teach people how we want to be treated. If you always let her interrupt you, then you're teaching your friend that you don't mind it, even though you do. Start teaching her it's not OK to interrupt you all the time. You don't have to make a big deal about it. Just say, "Sometimes when I'm talking, you start talking right in the middle of my sentence. Please stop doing that." Your friend may not be aware she has this habit. So smile and say, "I'll let you know next time it happens." And make sure you do!

Oh, and one more thing . . . if she interrupts you again, don't get angry and shout, "There! You see!? You're still doing it!!" That will just create a lot of stress in the friendship. Instead, stay cool and calm. Put up your hand and say, "Hold on. First let me finish what I'm saying." That ought to fix the problem.

Q9:

"What if my friend promises to sit with me at lunch, but she doesn't?"

A: Sometimes we make promises we really want to keep, but we forget or something else gets in the way. When that happens with a friend, you don't have to get upset, just remind her about her promise. That may fix the problem or it may not.

If your friend truly forgot her promise to sit with you, she may now have other plans that she can't get out of. Instead of feeling left out, find someone else to have lunch with today. It may not be easy, but you can do it. Later, talk things over with your friend, work it out, and agree to sit together tomorrow.

If this keeps happening, well, that's a different story. Sometimes people make *pretend promises* (promises they really don't mean.) If your friend continues offering up pretend promises, and you continue accepting them, then you'll be disappointed. If talking to her doesn't help, stop counting on her. Find other people who understand the importance of keeping a promise. They will become your new friends.

Q10:

"Friend A invited everyone to her party except Friend B. Friend B is mad at me for wanting to go. But I need to so I can be popular. Is it worth it?"

A: I understand that you want to go to the party, but if everyone was invited except Friend B, you can understand why she is upset. Maybe you can also understand why she is angry that you want to go without her.

When you say, "I need to go to the party so I can be popular," I wonder if the Popularity Game is more important to you than Friend B. People who ditch friends to be with more "popular" people often find themselves without any real friends.

Should you go to the party? If you do, then Friend B will probably be unhappy with you. She might get over it, but there is also a chance that your going to the party could really damage the friendship. You are the only one who can decide if it's worth the risk. To help you figure it out, think about this: If Friend B got invited and *you* didn't, how would you feel about her going without you? If it wouldn't feel right for her to go, then it's probably not right for you.

Friendship Quiz 1

Someone tells you that your friend did something bad. Do you:

[ ] A. Tell other people what you heard

[ ] B. Ask your friend if it's true

[ ] C. Ignore it

[ ] D. Stand up for your friend

[ ] E. Stay away from your friend, but don't tell her why

HINT: There may be more than one good solution!

ANSWERS:

A. **Not a good idea!** This is how rumors spread and people get hurt. It also adds to the "social garbage"—gossip, rumors, bullying & other kinds of mean behavior.

B. **Good thinking!** Friends talk *to* each other not *about* each other behind their backs.

C. **Smart move!** This is a good way to stop a rumor. You should also tell your friend what people are saying so she can defend herself.

D. **Well done!** Real friends stand up for each other. While you're at it, tell people that gossiping is hurtful.

E. **Not kind or respectful!** Real friends do not shut each other out; they talk to each other about what's going on.

Q11:

"*I have a few classmates that really annoy me. What should I do?*"

A: I'm wondering what these kids are doing that pushes your buttons and annoys you so much. If they are giggling and whispering about you or kicking your chair, then they're being disrespectful. Politely tell them, "Stop." If that doesn't work, then talk with your teacher about what's going on. Some kids might think that "tattling" is wrong, but really, if someone purposely tries to annoy you and won't stop when you ask, then it's wrong *not* to get the help you need.

If, on the other hand, you're "really annoyed" and your classmates are just doing their regular work, then become a detective and ask yourself, "Why does this annoy me so much?" Does it have to do with the way one of the kids looks? Or the way she talks? Or something else? If you need help figuring out why you are feeling so annoyed in class, please talk to your parents, your teacher, or the school counselor so you can get to the bottom of it.

Q12:

"A new girl from another country gets teased because she doesn't speak English. I want to be nice to her, but I'm afraid people will tease me. Should I be her friend?"

A: You already know the answer to your question, but you need some support. That's why I'm here. Yes, you should be her friend. She has come from far away to a place that is very strange to her and she needs a friend. Imagine how you'd feel moving to some place that's very different from what you're used to. What would it be like not to understand what people are saying and to have no one understand you? She's got a lot to deal with. Now imagine how she feels being teased. Having a friend like you could really help.

You say you're worried the teasers might turn on you. They might. Or they might become friendlier to the new girl when you show them the way. You have the chance to do something important, and you are brave enough to do it.

Be kind. Show this girl that people in your country can be very welcoming. You'll gain a new friend and learn amazing things about her and her culture.

Q13:

"What should I do if someone tattles on my friend?"

A: It sounds like you're thinking of "getting back" at the girl who got your friend in trouble. It's good to want to stand up for a friend, but it's not OK to hurt other people. Besides, this has nothing to do with you. When we put ourselves in the middle of things that aren't our business, we can make things worse.

"Tattling" is not always a bad thing. If someone is mean to you, then telling an adult is the right thing to do. Otherwise, the person might keep on being mean. Telling a trusted adult is also a smart way to be a good friend to yourself.

I don't know what really happened between this girl and your friend. Maybe you don't either. If your friend didn't do anything wrong, she can defend herself. If she did something that wasn't OK, then she has to make things right. You can't do that for her and you shouldn't try. I understand you want to support your friend, but my advice is that you stay out of this one.

Q14:

"What should I do when my friend gives me the Silent Treatment?"

A: I hate the Silent Treatment. It hurts when friends act like you don't count or that you aren't even there! When people treat you that way, you may start to believe there's something wrong with you. But there isn't! What's wrong here is the way your friend is acting. It's rude and mean.

You can't force someone to talk to you or to be a real friend. (You wouldn't want to force her even if you could!) But you should remind yourself that you deserve to be treated with respect. Giving someone the silent treatment is not respectful. If anyone does this to you, say, "STOP this Silent Treatment. You're being mean." Your words might wake up your friend. Or they may wake up other kids who are also being mean. If the rudeness continues, then shop around for nicer people to hang out with.

Another tip, since you know how awful it feels to be ignored, please don't ever give anyone the silent treatment! No matter how mad you are, everyone deserves respect.

Q15:

"My bff is mad because she wanted to do something bad and I said no because I knew it was wrong. She got away with it, but she still hates me."

A: I'm proud of you for not letting your bff pressure you to do something wrong. This shows that you are a strong girl who knows how to think for herself and make healthy choices. That's not always easy when friends are pushing and pulling you in other directions, but you did it!

Your bff doesn't really hate you. She's probably angry because you didn't go along with her idea. And even though she didn't get caught, she may feel guilty about what she did. She may wish she had listened to you. If that's true, she may be using anger to keep you away, so she won't have to talk or think about the mistake she made.

Give her time to cool off. You two may become best friends again. If she has more ideas that don't feel right, stay strong and tell her what you think. Maybe you can help her make better choices. But if she's not listening to you, then look for a new friend. If you stay with this one, hanging out with her could get you into trouble.

How to be a Super Friend

"If you've done something wrong, apologize. Don't say, 'I'm sorry, *but* . . .' That makes things worse. Say, 'I'm sorry I was rude to you.' Then don't do the same mistake again."
    —Chantelle, 14

"Let your friend know if she isn't respecting you. If she gets mad about that, then she's not a true friend."
    —Emma, 13

"If you and your friend have a big fight, go home and punch a pillow to calm down. Losing control makes things worse."
    —Harper, 13

"Make sure *you* aren't being too overpowering, because nobody likes being a doormat."
    —Nikki, 13

"If you're having a tough time, remember *that's* what friends are for, to help you."
    —Zoe, 12

Q16:

"I'm kinda shy, so how do I make new friends?"

A: Every girl has moments when she's ready to jump right into the middle of something new. And every girl also has moments when she feels shy. That's normal. It's also normal to want friends. Try these ways to make new friends:

- Think of your shyness as a *part* of you, but not *all* of who you are.

- Make a list of the things you like about yourself. For example, "I'm a good soccer player." Or "I'm good at science."

- Say to yourself: "I'm a nice girl. I'm going to give more people a chance to get to know me. If I do that, they'll want to be my friend."

- Give yourself a challenge to smile and say "Hi" to five new kids every day. (If that's too many, start with one or two.) When friendly smiles start coming back at you, you'll feel more confident.

- Join an afterschool activity. Doing something you enjoy, with other people, is a great way to make new friends.

Good luck!

Q17:

"My best friend is always showing off and thinks she is the best at everything. It's annoying."

A: When we show off, it's not usually because we think we're "the best at everything." We show off because we all want other people to like us and sometimes we worry that no one will if we don't brag about ourselves.

You might be a person who never brags. But now that you understand more about why your friend might be doing it, you two can have a good conversation about showing off and how it makes you feel. Tell her that you and others like her just the way she is. Maybe she'll realize that she doesn't need to show off so much.

If that doesn't help, here's something else that might: When she starts doing her thing, simply walk away. Think of it as turning off a TV show you're not interested in. If your friend asks you why you left, calmly say, "It bothers me when you do that. It feels like showing off."

Q18:

"My friend always says she's busy with her family, but I know she's really with her new friends. It makes me want to cry or punch something or someone."

A: You're sad because you're missing your friend and you wish you could go back to the time when it was just you two having fun together. You're also feeling a little jealous of her new friends. Punching something (or someone) isn't going to solve this problem. Neither is crying. But changing your thinking may help.

Did you have a different best friend, in the past? If so, then you know friendships can change. Sometimes we feel close to certain people, then after a while we may start to feel closer to other people. That's what seems to be happening. Right now, your friend wants to spend more time with her new friends than with you. It's just the way she feels.

Instead of feeling sorry for yourself, look for a new best friend. First make a list of what you want in a friend, then start shopping for one today! I'm sure you will find someone who wants to be your friend as much as you want to be hers.

Q19:

"My best friend and I have a crush on the same boy!"

A: When two friends have a crush on the same person, they may feel jealous of each other. They worry whether the crush likes one of them more. Sometimes they stop acting like friends. But that doesn't have to happen!

Talk to your friend about how you've both changed since this crush started. Hopefully you can calm down and stop competing for this boy's attention. This isn't really a competition at all because the boy isn't a prize. He's a human being. He's got his own feelings and his own thoughts about whether he even wants a girlfriend. He may like both of you as friends. Or he may not actually know either of you well enough to have any feelings for you. If that's true, then you girls are getting upset over nothing.

Be smart and do not risk hurting your friendship over a boy. Crushes come and go, but if you take care of the friendship, you and your best friend may be close to each other for a very long time.

Q20:

"Whenever I tell my best friend something exciting, she makes it not so exciting. :O(
Like she says, 'So what?'"

A: Sharing good news and knowing some- one else is happy for you is one of the coolest things about having a friend. But when a friend gives you a big "So what?" it's like showing her your new, beautiful, red balloon and instead of being excited, she pops it!! You're left with nothing but a busted balloon and hurt feelings.

If your friend can count on you when she's excited or when she needs cheering up, then you are a good friend to her. But if you can't count on *her*, then you are giving more than you are getting in this friendship.

Be a real friend to yourself. Instead of letting her pop your balloon again and again, talk to her. Help her understand how it feels when you tell her something cool and she brushes it aside. This can help her learn to be a better friend. It can also help you set higher standards for what you need in a best friend.

FRIENDSHIP QUIZ 2

Your friend tells you that a certain girl is "weird" and you shouldn't be her friend. Do you:

[ ] A. Stay away from the other girl

[ ] B. Tell the other girl what your friend said about her

[ ] C. Get to know the girl better and form your own opinion

[ ] D. Tell other people that the girl is "weird"

[ ] E. Ask your friend why she thinks that

Answers:

A. **Not smart.** If you do that, then you're letting your friend do your thinking for you.

B. **Oh no!** This turns people into enemies. It's better to be a Peacemaker.

C. **Smart move!** Use your own judgment in deciding who will be your friend.

D. **Not helpful!** This is how bullying becomes an even bigger problem.

E. **Great thinking!** Asking questions is a good way to learn more. That will help you make better decisions.

Q21:

"When my friend does weird things I don't say anything. But when I do something (like a funny dance) she yells at me. I want to tell her I don't like that, but I don't want to be mean, like her."

A: I think it's awesome that you accept your friend for who she is and do not put her down when she does any of her "weird" things. You deserve the same respect from her. She shouldn't yell at you when you dance, especially since you're not trying to hurt or embarrass her. You're just feeling free and joyful, and that's good.

I don't know for certain, but maybe your friend gets upset because she's worried that other girls will tease you about your dancing or that someone will tease *her* for being your friend! When we are scared or worried, we aren't always as kind as we should be. But that's no excuse for being rude.

When you feel like dancing, go ahead and dance. If your friend has a problem with that, then talk to her about it. Maybe you can help her lighten up. But whatever you do, please, do *not* stop being yourself. It's the best thing about you.

Q22:

"Every time me and my friend have a private conversation, this new girl pulls my friend away. What should I do?"

A: It sounds like the new girl has a strong personality, but she doesn't have all the power in this situation. Your friend has power that she isn't really using. If she didn't want to get pulled away she could tell the girl to stop. And you have power too. You could tell your friend how you feel. Real friends tell each other the truth. You might say something like this: "I don't like how ____ pulls you away from me. How come you let her do that?" Listen to her side of it. Work together to figure out a way through this. Either your friend will stand up for herself or she'll let herself be pulled away. Her choice.

You also have choices. You can invite your friend over so the two of you have time together, outside of school. At school, you can either stand there watching the two of them go off together or you can make some new friends.

Think about this too: It's not easy being the new kid. She wants a friend and doesn't know a more polite way to get one. Maybe the three of you could be friends. That's worth a try!

Q23:

"I had some friends over and didn't invite one girl, then she found out!"

A: No rule says everyone has to be invited to everything. But here's rule #1 in this friendship book: *It's never OK to be cruel.*

There are times we get invited to parties and things. There are also times when each of us gets left out. Being left out is not always fair or easy to deal with. Part of growing up is accepting that. Another part is learning to be kind and respectful of other people's feelings. The girl you didn't invite is probably upset. If you've ever been left out, you know the feeling.

If she asks why she wasn't invited, what will you say? Some adults might tell you to make an excuse. ("My Mom said I could only invite four people and you were number five.") Unless that's true, don't pretend it is. Instead you might say, "I didn't mean to hurt your feelings." Then you can have a conversation about why you didn't invite her. You might say something like this, "I didn't invite you because I haven't been feeling very close to you lately." Whatever you say, be respectful of her feelings. That's how you'd want someone to treat you.

Q24:

"What *do* I do when people are playing a game and don't include me?"

A: I'm sorry you're feeling left out. Take some slow deep breaths to calm down. Breathe in. Breathe out. (Go ahead. I'll wait.)

Better? OK. Now listen. What if this game is only for a certain number of players? If that's it, then ask if you can play the next round. Hopefully the answer is "yes!" Meanwhile, cheer from the sidelines or find other people to play with until it's your turn.

Another possibility: they didn't want to include you. Some kids turn their games into little clubs and try to hurt other kids by keeping them out. Not cool! If that's what is going on here, you can:

A. Talk with them, calmly and respectfully

B. Talk with a teacher about it

C. Look for other people to play with

D. Feel sorry for yourself and waste your whole recess being in a bad mood

A, B, and C are good choices. D is not. You're not helpless. Make your own fun by reaching out to other good-hearted classmates. Then you won't feel so left out.

Q25:

"My friend gets mad at me a lot. I don't know why, but I'm afraid to talk to her about it."

A: Friendships should be fun and caring. This one sounds like a scary movie.

You don't know why she gets angry and I don't either. She may have gotten into a bad habit of yelling when she doesn't get her way. Or she may be hurting inside because people at home yell at her. Whatever the reason, yelling at people isn't OK. It has to stop.

I understand why you're scared to talk to her. But if you *could* talk to her, you might say, "I don't like it when you yell at me. Real friends shouldn't do that to each other." That may give her something to think about.

If you don't want to talk to her about it, talk to an adult you trust. If your friend's behavior doesn't change, take a break from this drama.

Find at least one kind girl or boy to be your recess buddy. If your friend wants you to play with her, calmly say, "Sorry. I'm playing with_____ today." This could help her realize what happens when she treats people badly.

How to be a Super Friend

"If you and your friend have a problem, talk about it. Because no matter how much you want it to go away, if you do nothing it won't."
—Inez, 15

"Be yourself. If you act like someone you're not, you may end up being friends with someone you don't get on with. So be normal. :-)"
—Sonya, 14

"You and your friend don't have to agree with each other on everything. Don't get into a huge debate. Respect each other's differences."
—Cassidy, 15

"Let your friends see that you really appreciate and need them in life."
—Tawanda, 13

"Be genuine and don't try and fit in if you're not comfortable with it. People see right through that."
—Michelle, 14

Q26:

"My bff is not always nice, but I've known her forever. How do I decide if I should keep her as a friend or find a new one?"

A: Imagine you've had a special t-shirt for a long time. You really like some things about it: It's purple! It feels soft! And some things aren't so great: It's got a stain that won't come out. It's a little tight.

How do you decide whether to keep the shirt? Make a PROs and CONs list! PRO = Good reasons to keep the t-shirt. CON = Good reasons to give away the t-shirt. This can help you decide what to do. Making lists can also help you figure out other things, like whether to stay in a friendship or take a break.

Fold a blank piece of paper in half the long way. Write PRO at the top of the left column and CON on the right. On the PRO side make a list of good reasons to keep this friend. On the CON side make a list of good reasons to find a new friend. Now, take a look at both lists. How do you feel about making a decision now? Remember, you can also take the "middle road" and choose to spend less time with your old friend and find a new one too!

Q27:

"Me and my bff always fight. She distracts me in class and she is ruining me! How do I get out of this friendship?"

A: You're having a hard time not being distracted by your bff. The next time it happens, look her in the eye and whisper "Stop!" If she continues, do not respond. Hopefully she will get the message that you won't talk to her during class. If that doesn't work, ask the teacher for help.

Even without the distractions, it sounds like you don't want to be in this friendship anymore. That's OK. You have the right to end it, but you don't have the right to be mean. Talk to her privately and say something like this, "Lately we've been fighting a lot and I don't feel as close to you as I used to. Maybe you feel the same way. We're not bringing out the best in each other, so I'm going to take a vacation from this friendship."

Don't make plans with her anymore, but don't talk behind her back. And make sure you're always polite when you see her. You will make other friends and she will too

Q28:

"When I asked my friend something she went 'Shhhhh!!!' A minute later she asked what I wanted, and I said 'Shhh!' I was just kidding, but we haven't talked since."

A: Your friend may have started this fight, but you made things worse by "shushing" her back. Part of you was just kidding, but part of you did it to get back at her because you were hurt. There was anger in your "Shhh!" and she felt it. It would have been more respectful if you had taken a moment to calm down. Luckily, it's not too late to make things better.

If you feel that the friendship is worth saving, then talk to her honestly. You might say something like this, "When you shushed me I got mad so I shushed you back. Then you got mad. I guess nobody likes being shushed!" Then you could ask, "Why did you shush me in the first place?" Talk about it. This is how two friends can get past their anger and repair a break in a friendship.

For extra fun: After you and your friend have made up, you might have a "play-fight" and take turns shushing each other. You'll probably end up laughing!

Q29:

"My best friend doesn't like me doing anything on my own. I love art and when I don't have time to do it, I don't feel like I'm really me!"

A: Best friends do not need to do everything together. You are both allowed to have time away from each other. It's cool to be on your own to do whatever you like. Independence is a good thing.

It sounds like your friend doesn't understand yet how important "on my own" time is to you. Maybe she doesn't get it because it's not the same for her. Or maybe you've never explained to her how much you love doing art. You might say something like this, "Sometimes, when I feel like drawing, I don't want to talk or do anything else but draw. When I'm in one of those drawing moods, I want you to just leave me alone and let me draw without getting upset."

You might also ask her what she likes to do when she's on her own. This kind of conversation can help the two of you understand each other better. That can help your friendship become stronger.

Q30:

"When my best friend is with me and other girls, she acts like I'm invisible. I want to tell her, but I'm scared."

A: Treating someone like he or she is invisible is so rude. You aren't invisible. You are right here and you need to tell your friend that you are not letting her treat you this way any more. You might feel a little scared to talk to her about it, but you have to. Staying silent isn't going to fix this problem. Silence sends a message that you're OK with what's she's doing. You don't want to send that message because it's not true!

Talk to your friend privately. It doesn't have to be a big dramatic scene. Just tell her, calmly and respectfully, that the way she acts makes you very uncomfortable, and that you are wondering if she is really your friend. Then close your mouth and *listen* to what she says. If she makes excuses or blames you or acts like she doesn't know what you're talking about, then it is time to take a vacation from this friendship. Reach out to other people and get the kind of friendship you want and need. And please try to remember to *be* a good friend everyone.

FRIENDSHIP QUIZ 3

Your bff says she's mad at you, but won't tell you why. Do you:

[ ] A. Keep asking her, "Why are you mad at me? Why?! TELL ME!!!"

[ ] B. Give her some space

[ ] C. Ask another friend why your bff is mad

[ ] D. Tell other girls that your bff is being mean to you

[ ] E. Become a detective and examine the clues: When did this start? What was going on? Who said what? etc.

ANSWERS:

A. **Not a great plan.** That can be annoying. Besides you can't force someone to talk.

B. **Sounds good!** Some people need time to cool down before they feel like talking about why they're upset.

C. **That could work.** Sometimes other friends can help when someone is too angry to talk.

D. **Don't go there!** Talking behind her back will probably make your bff even madder.

E. **Good use of your brain!** Thinking about this problem calmly can provide hints about what's going on.

Q31:

"My friends make fun of my hair and my feet . . . but they say they're just kidding. What should I do?"

A: Teasing can easily become a *slippery slope*. Do you know what that means? A comment may start off as a harmless little joke then quickly slips and slides downhill, going faster, and causing more hurt and embarrassment.

Playful teasing between friends is OK only if *everyone* is OK with it. You don't like the teasing, so your friends need to stop. And you need to start taking better care of yourself by speaking up when things don't feel right.

The next time they make fun of you, say, "Hey, cut it out!" If they say, "Just kidding!" tell them, "It doesn't feel like kidding. It hurts. If we are really friends, then you won't do it anymore."

Another way to handle this: Everyone has at least one thing he or she hates being teased about. Protect your feelings by building an imaginary "No Kidding Zone" around that thing. Then you and your friends agree not to tease each other about anything in The Zone. If someone forgets the rule, instead of feeling bad or getting angry, just say, "NKZ" (No Kidding Zone). That should help.

Q32:

"My friend and I aren't interested in the same stuff anymore. I'm not mad at her, I'm just kinda bored."

A: Have you ever loved a pair of shoes until one day you put them on and *ouch!!* They no longer fit because you've outgrown them. We can outgrow friendships too. If you used to have a best friend that you're not so close with anymore, then you know how that can happen. It's easier when both friends move on at the same time. But when one moves on and the other feels left behind, it can hurt.

Maybe you've outgrown this friendship. Talk to your friend. Say something like this, "I care about you, but I'm changing. Now when we're together, it feels like we're interested in different things, so it's not so much fun. I want to take a vacation from this friendship." You don't need to make pretend promises or feel guilty about wanting time away from her. It's OK for friends to have time apart. Just calmly tell her the truth, and give her a chance to talk about her feelings while you listen.

It will be ok. You will both make other friends. And who knows? Someday this friendship may be a good fit again. That can happen too.

Q33:

"My friend is *so* nice and *so* beautiful
everybody loves her and compliments her
all the time. I just can't stop being jealous."

A: Jealousy is a powerful emotion. We all feel it at times and it's never fun. Your feelings of jealousy are building walls between you and your friend. That's not fair because your friend hasn't done anything wrong.

Jealous thoughts are like a bad habit, popping into your head whenever you look at your friend or think about her. You say you can't stop being jealous, but you really *can*.

Here's how: Pretend you've got an imaginary net to catch jealous thoughts. When you notice yourself thinking, "She's *so* beautiful! Everybody loves her!" use your net and say to yourself, "Gotcha, jealous thought! Be gone." Picture the trapped thought shrinking to nothing and disappearing. *Poof!* Then smile and be proud of yourself because you just won a mini-battle with the Jealousy Monster.

Keep catching those thoughts while remembering what you like about yourself. This will help you become a happier, calmer person, and a much better friend.

Q34:

"When my friends (A & B) see my other friend (C) they run . . . and so do I. I don't want to hurt anyone, but I feel stuck."

A: You feel "stuck" because you don't know what to do. It can be confusing when you want to do two things at the same time. It can be really confusing if someone will be upset with you no matter what you choose.

You want to run off with A & B so they will be happy with you. You also want to stay with C so she will be happy with you. You have a good heart. You know it isn't right to run away from a friend. If someone did that to you, you'd be upset.

Part of you probably wishes the four of you could be happy friends together. That would be nice, wouldn't it? Suggest it to A & B. If they don't like your idea, then here's how to get un-stuck from this situation: The next time A & B run away, be a real friend and stay with C. If A & B tease you or try to pull you away, say, "No. I'm not playing that run away game anymore. It's mean." That will help C and it will also give A & B something important to think about. It will also make you proud of the girl you are.

Q35:

"My bff is mad because I hugged some-one she really hates. How can I get her to be my friend again?"

A: Your friend is trying to be your boss and she has made up a little test for you. Here's what she's thinking, "If you hate the girl I hate, then you are my friend. If you like the girl I hate, then I hate you too."

You want to be her friend, but what do you think about this test? It doesn't feel like something a real friend would do.

If you believe that you have to hate everyone she hates, then you can say you're sorry and promise never to hug anyone again without your bff's permission. You would pass her friendship test and she'd be happy with you . . . for now.

Before you promise, ask yourself: "Is giving someone a friendly hug something I need to apologize for?" I don't think so! Hugging is a good thing. If you apologize, you might never feel comfortable hugging anyone without your bff's permission. You don't need anyone's permission to be the friendly girl you are.

Here's to more hugs!

HOW TO BE A SUPER FRIEND

"Don't bully people because they're different."
—Zafira, 13

"If you're mad at your friend, write a note, but don't give it her. Hide it under your pillow. Much later re-read the note. Was what you wrote really fair? Was it rude or mean? Try to forgive your friend or call a truce until you can talk about it calmly."
—Kasey, 14

"When a friend has a problem, try and help the same way you'd want people to help you."
—Yoshiko, 12

"All friends fight, but don't let one fight ruin your friendship."
—Lily, 14

"If you and your friend have a fight, talk it out. Stay quiet and the whole thing will blow up. You'll start ignoring each other."
—Brianna, 16

Q36:

"I'm a very smart girl, but I'm deaf in one ear and my speech is not that clear. I work hard to correct it, but I get teased a lot. It's hard to make friends when no one gives me a chance."

A: This teasing has to stop. It's so disrespectful. Your parents should set up a meeting with your teacher, the principal, the teasers, and *their* parents. Everyone needs to know what's going on and what each person can do to make your school a friendlier place.

Maybe your classmates have never known someone who is deaf or hard of hearing. Maybe your speech seems strange to them, so they are a little afraid of you. That sounds silly, but sometimes people are afraid of things they're not used to. And fear spreads quickly. I'll bet your classmates would like you if they gave themselves a chance to know you.

I wish I could wave a magic wand so all kids would see that each of us is "different" in some way. Different doesn't mean "bad" or "weird" or "broken." But I don't have a wand. Still, change is possible. You've worked hard on your speech. Use that same determination to find a real friend. Pick the nicest person in your class. Ask the adult who takes care of you if you two can set up a playdate. Good luck!

Q37:

"This girl was mean to me and now she's trying to be my friend again. I'm not sure if I should trust her."

A: After someone has been mean to you, it makes sense to wonder, "Should I trust her again?" That voice inside your head can help you take care of yourself. But since this girl seems to want to be your friend again, maybe she's sorry for what she did and would like a second chance.

Have you ever made a mistake and wished for a second chance? I know I sure have! Before you give her one, you have to talk to her about what happened before. That's an important part of re-building a friendship. She needs to apologize for hurting you. After she apologizes, you might say, "If we are going to be friends again, you have to show that I can trust you." Then watch and see what she does.

If she becomes a real friend, then giving her a second chance was a good choice. She will have learned something important and your friendship will be stronger. But if she goes back to being mean, then take a break right away, because no one has the right to treat you that way.

Q38:

"My friends peer pressured me into playing a mean trick on my other friend. Now I feel guilty."

A: You gave in to the pressure to do something mean because you wanted your friends to like you. We all want people to like us, but it's never OK to be mean. The guilt you feel is your Inner Voice reminding you that you made a mistake. Thinking about mistakes helps us make fewer of them.

Saying you were "peer pressured" makes it sound like you blame your friends for what you did. You always have the choice to do the right thing. Instead of going along with the trick, what could you have done? You could have said, "That's not a good idea." Or "No. That's mean!" That would have made you a good leader and a good friend. It would also give the others something to think about. If they still wanted to be mean, you could have helped your other friend.

If you want to lose the guilt and feel proud of yourself again, then apologize to your friend for what you did. Hopefully she will forgive you. If she gives you another chance, do your best to be a real friend.

Q39:

"My bff is planning to do something really mean to my ex-bff who once did something mean to me. I feel like warning my ex-bff. Should I?"

A: Your bff probably thinks she is helping you "get back" at your ex-bff for what happened before. Your bff is not thinking clearly, but it sounds like you are. I'm very proud of you for realizing that this plan is wrong. It's just going to create more mean-ness, anger and hurt feelings in the world. I call this kind of stuff "social garbage." It messes up schools and friendships. Kids don't need more social garbage they need *less.*

Here's how you can help: Talk to your bff right away. Since she hasn't done anything yet, you still have a chance to stop her. Tell her, "I know you are trying to help me, but I don't want this kind of help. Being mean is wrong. Don't do anything to hurt my ex-bff."

If you are strong and clear you can probably convince your bff to dump the plan. If she says she's going to do it anyway, then warn the other girl. That's the right thing to do.

Q40:

"I'm a different race than my friends. Their hair is curly and bouncy but mine's so straight it just hangs. I feel left out. It's stupid, but I want to be a part of them!"

A: When girls write to me about getting teased, their emails make me sad because teasing hurts and no one has the right to hurt anyone. But you don't say that your friends are teasing you. In a way, you are teasing *yourself!* You do that every time you think "My hair's so straight it just hangs!" When you put yourself down, you're not being a good friend . . . to you!

You say it's "stupid" to worry about what kind of hair you have, so you already know these negative thoughts are not helpful. I agree! We are happiest when we like ourselves for who we are instead of wishing we were different.

Here's a reminder that may help you stop worrying: You don't need to look like anyone else to be awesome. And you don't need to look like your friends to be "part of them." They already love you just the way you are. It's time to love yourself more. You are super special. In fact, you are the only one in the entire universe who can be you. Go for it!

FRIENDSHIP QUIZ 4

Your bff made another friend and now she is being mean to you. You have cried about this . . . a lot. Do you:

[ ] A. Stay away from her

[ ] B. Give her a present and try to get her to like you again

[ ] C. Keep on crying

[ ] D. Hang out with other friends

[ ] E. Be mean back to her

ANSWERS:

A. **That makes sense.** You will be happier staying away from anyone who is mean to you.

B. **Not a good plan.** Real friends are nice to each other because they *want* to be, not because they get a gift.

C. **Don't do that.** You've already cried enough and nothing changed. Wash your face and do something to make at least one new friend.

D. **Good thinking!** You deserve to hang out with people who want to be your friends.

E. **Skip that idea!** More meanness will only add to the social garbage without making you any happier.

Q41:

"What *do* you do if you're in a fight and you want to get out of it?"

A: It takes only one angry person to start a fight, but it takes two angry people to continue it.

Maybe when this fight started, you were so angry you really got into it. But now it sounds like you have had enough fighting. You want to make peace. Good! You have the power to do it, because it only takes one person to end a fight. You can be that person.

How do you make peace? By being peaceful! Talk to the girl you're fighting with. Say, "I've had enough of this fight. I'm not going to fight with you anymore." She may try to keep the fight going by teasing you, acting mean, and talking behind your back. She might also try to turn other girls against you. But really, if you just hold your head up and decide that you are not going to let her pull you back into the "boxing ring," then you will be fine. It would also be a good idea to try to find at least one kind person to be your friend—someone who will stand with you as a Peacemaker.

Q42:

"How do I stop being a third wheel with my two friends?"

A: When it comes to close friends being together at the same time, and getting along with each other, often it's best when there are only two. Why not three or four? Maybe it's just easier to have a conversation between two people because there are only two opinions to consider. Two people might also have an easier time making plans because there are fewer phone calls to make and fewer parents to get permission from.

It could be that your two friends just really enjoy being together. They're probably not aware of how you've been feeling. Talk to them about it. You might say, "When you two are together, I feel like you don't need me. That makes me feel left out." (If you're not sure you can say that, ask your favorite adult to "practice" with you until you're comfortable saying what you need to say.) If things don't get better, spend time with each of these friends separately. If that doesn't work, shop for a new friend who doesn't already have a bff. You and your new friend may form your own twosome.

Q43:

"How can I talk to my friend about why she's mad at me if she refuses to talk?"

A: It sounds like your friend is really angry and she's blaming you for something you did or something she thinks you did. You can't solve this problem on your own. You need to work together to get to the bottom of what's going on. But it's impossible for two people to have a real conversation if both of them aren't willing to talk to each other and listen with respect.

If your friend has had time to cool off and she's still not talking to you, then maybe you could write her an email or a letter. Keep the message simple, like this, "I don't know why you're mad at me. I don't want to lose our friendship, so we need to talk about this."

If she doesn't write back and still won't talk to you, then maybe you should take a break from the drama and move on. Try to make some new friends who understand that all friends have problems from time to time, but real friends do their best to work through a problem . . . together.

Q44:

"One of my friends bosses and bullies the other. How do I tell her it's wrong?"

A: You have a good heart, but that's not enough to make friendships better. You also need courage. Since you are friends with both girls, use your friendship power for good.

Talk to the friend who is being bullied. Tell her what you've noticed and give her a pep talk. You might say something like this, "You shouldn't let ____ boss you around. If you don't tell her to STOP, she'll keep doing it."

Talk privately to your "bossy" friend. Take a deep breath and say something like this: "You're my friend, but when you're mean to ____ I lose respect for you." Then close your mouth and listen to what she has to say. If she acts like she has no idea what you're talking about, give her an example. Hopefully she will get the message and change her ways. If not, change *yours*. The next time she bullies anyone, speak up. If that doesn't make things better, you and your friend need to spend less time with the bossy girl.

Q45:

"My bff is spreading rumors about me, telling my new friends that I'm a mean girl. I'm not! But she doesn't care."

A: You're wrong. She cares a lot! That's why she's spreading nasty rumors about you. That sounds mixed up, doesn't it? But your bff is so worried about losing you to your new friends that she isn't thinking clearly at all. (That can happen when we feel jealous or angry.)

This gossip has to stop. Please talk to your bff. You might say something like this, "I know you've been talking about me to my new friends. I still want you and me to be friends, but I don't want you talking about me behind my back. Please stop doing that because it's really upsetting me."

Those are powerful words and they could be like a magic key unlocking a door. Your bff's worries and fears are hiding behind that door. She's scared of losing you. If you've ever lost a friend, maybe you can understand. It sounds like she needs reassuring. How might you help her stop worrying?

How to be a Super Friend

"When you and your friend have a fight, do not involve other people or take sides in other people's fights. This makes everything worse than it needs to be."
          —Kalea, 15

"Open your heart and understand your friends' feelings so they'll know you care about them."
          —Mari, 13

"Be cool. Don't worry too much. People come and go, but the people who care for you will always stay with you no matter what."
          —Felicity, 14

"Don't spread secrets. It will make things worse and worse."
          —Daisy, 12

"Through all the ups and downs, there will be a few people who stay; your true friends."
          —Kirsten, 14

Q46:

"Me and my ex-bff got into a fight. Now she's stealing all my other friends!"

A: You are worried and scared that your friends will join your ex-bff's side and turn against you! Maybe some of that has already started to happen. But the way you're thinking about this is a little mixed up.

You say your ex-bff is "stealing" your friends. That's not possible. Stealing is taking an object that's not yours and walking away with it without permission. Objects can be stolen, but people are not objects. A friend can't be "stolen." Your friends make their own choices. No one is "stealing" anyone, so please stop thinking about it like that.

Because you're upset you need to talk to your friends about what's going on. Do not make them choose between you and your ex-bff. They don't have to choose. They have the right to be friends with you, or with your ex-bff, or with both of you.

If you feel like you need more friends, then reach out to new people. Choose wisely and continue being the best friend you know how to be to all your friends.

Q47:

"I'm the new girl and I need some friends."

A: Welcome to your new school! You're probably excited and a little sad because you left some friends behind. Being in a new school without friends is like watching a movie without popcorn. Making new friends will help you feel more at home in your new home. But how do you make new friends? Here are some tips:

1. **Be friendly.** That means act like someone who *wants* friends. Smile. Say, "Hi, I'm ____. What's your name?" That lets kids know what a nice girl you are.

2. **Be a good listener.** Ask kids what this new school is like and *listen* to what they say. When people ask *you* questions, don't brag ("I was the most popular girl at my old school.") or make stuff up ("My old school had flying unicorns kids could ride on.")

3. **Ask to be included.** This takes courage, so you may need some slow deep breaths before you say, "Hi. Can I play?"

4. **Find a buddy.** Be on the lookout for someone who seems like he or she could become a good friend. Use tip #1.

Good luck and have fun!

Q48:

"My friend is moving away really soon! I am so sad. What should I do to keep our friendship strong?"

A: It's sad when someone you care about moves away. Not seeing each other every day changes a friendship, but not necessarily in a bad way. Think of it like this: when you're always together there may not be much to talk about at the end of the day. But when you go to different schools, you will have lots to share with each other when you talk or email or video chat.

You could also write letters (the old fashioned kind, using pen and paper). Or you could both keep a journal and every few days mail a page to each other. If you like to draw, you could decorate the pages and the envelope too. Think how cool it will be every time a letter arrives in your mailbox. Talk to your friend about the idea. If you both like it, try it!

Please remember that you've got what it takes to be a great friend, so use it to make some new ones. They won't replace your old friend, you'll just add them to your friendship circle.

Q49:

"My bff is super sensitive and gets super upset. How do I avoid hurting her feelings when *everything* hurts her feelings?"

A: Part of the problem may be that "super sensitive" people, like your friend, get their feelings hurt easily. Because you never know what will upset her, being her friend can sometimes feel a little scary, as if you were a mouse tiptoeing around, trying not to wake up a sleeping cat!

When you are with her, I'm sure you are always very careful choosing your words. But sometimes, even when we're trying to be very nice and not at all mean, our words may hurt people anyway. It happens.

Instead of worrying about not upsetting your friend, talk to her. You might say something like this, "I never mean to upset you, but sometimes when I say something, your feelings get hurt and I feel really bad. What can we both do, so this doesn't happen as much?"

Friends who talk about misunderstandings do a better job understanding each other and taking care of the friendship.

FRIENDSHIP QUIZ 5

You don't have a bff right now and you're happy being friends with lots of girls. But people tell you that *everyone* needs a bff. Do you:

[ ] A. Tell them it's not true

[ ] B. Ignore what they say

[ ] C. Wonder if they are right

[ ] D. Start looking for a bff

[ ] E. Worry that there's something wrong with you

ANSWERS:

A. **Good idea!** Since you're happy without a bff, then tell them it's not true that "everyone" needs one.

B. **Makes good sense.** People say lots of things that aren't true. No need to respond to this.

C. **You could do that.** Sometimes what people say makes us think about things in new ways. That can helpful.

D. **Sure.** But only if you really want a bff, not because someone says you need one.

E. **Not necessary!** There's nothing "wrong" with you. Don't let other people's opinions bring you down. Be yourself and be confident.

Q50:

"Why are people mean to each other?"

A: Great question! Sometimes we feel like hurting other people because we feel left out or jealous. Being mean is never OK, so when we're upset we have to try to calm down and think things through so nobody gets hurt. That's not always easy because feelings and thoughts move so quickly. Sometimes it just takes one word or a certain look from someone and BAM! We're angry and not thinking clearly. Maybe we believe that being mean will make us feel more powerful. That's a mistake. Being mean often makes us feel smaller and much less proud of who we are.

"Social garbage" is a real problem. There's a lot of it in every school and not enough real friendship. When girls and boys *add* to the garbage by being mean, people get hurt. I'm just sick of it. You probably are too. That's why I'm looking for solutions from smart, kind, brave girls like you. **What can you do to be a better friend to yourself and every-one else? Think about it and share your ideas at GirlsQandA.com**

About the Author

ANNIE FOX is an internationally respected parenting expert and trusted online advisor to girls of all ages. She teaches girls to effectively manage their emotions so they can think more clearly and act with more compassion and respect. Her award-winning work includes the groundbreaking Middle School Confidential book and app series for tweens and *Teaching Kids to Be Good People: Progressive Parenting for the 21st Century*. She's also the host of the popular weekly podcast, *Family Confidential: Secrets of Successful Parenting*. Since 1997, when she launched groundbreaking teen website The InSite, Annie has been answering teen and parenting questions from around the world. She is a sought-after speaker who takes equal delight connecting with students, educators, and parents.

Annie may be reached through her website, AnnieFox.com

ABOUT THE ILLUSTRATOR

ERICA DE CHAVEZ is a girl who designs picture books by day and is a visual storyteller by night who has a *slight* obsession for pandas, bows, and the color purple. Growing up, she was never the prettiest nor the most popular girl in middle school, but she never let that stop her from being the loud, passionate, and fun-loving artist she still is today.

Originally from Kissimmee, Florida, Erica now lives and creates art in Brooklyn, New York. She hopes that her artwork can touch the hearts of those in need of a smile and a good laugh. *The Girls' Q&A Book on Friendship* is her first illustrated publication.

Learn more about her and her artwork at PandaErica.com

ABOUT THE PUBLISHER

ELECTRIC EGGPLANT was founded in 1992 by David and Annie Fox, Electric Eggplant has been on the forefront of multimedia design and production. In their 40 years of marriage, they've partnered on dozens of trailblazing projects, including co-founding the Marin Computer Center (1977)—the world's first public-access microcomputer center. They've also co-produced two award-winning children. The Foxes have consistently garnered kudos for their work on games, educational software, Emotional Intelligence content, as well as books and apps for kids, tweens, and teens.

David began his career in game design in 1982 as employee #3 at Lucasfilm Games (LucasArts). His latest game is *Rube Works: The Official Rube Goldberg Invention Game* for desktop and mobile. For the younger set, Electric Eggplant produces the Raymond and Sheila series written by Annie Fox and illustrated by Eli Noyes, and *People Are Like Lollipops* written by Annie Fox and illustrated by Brian Narelle.

Learn more about Electric Eggplant at ElectricEggplant.com